Introduction

Donald J. Goergen, O.P.

In the year of Our Lord, 1216, the Order of Preachers was formally established. St. Dominic had received the final approval from Pope Honorius III. In 2016 the Order will celebrate 800 years of preaching the gospel of Our Lord Jesus Christ. In 1939, the Province of St. Albert the Great, USA, was established, which celebrated its 75th anniversary in 2014. On that occasion, in January, at their annual Provincial Assembly, the brothers of the province gathered to say thank you for all that has been, and for all that is to come, yes, to borrow an expression of Dag Hammarskjöld's, the United Nations second Secretary-General and a recipient of the Nobel Peace Prize. They were treated with three excellent presentations and also thereby challenged to look to their future. Michael Mascari, O.P., himself a son of the Province of St. Albert the Great, and a former Provincial of the province, currently serving as Socius for Studies to the Master of the Order; Joseph Tobin, C.Ss.R., Archbishop of Indianapolis; and Dr. Scott Appleby, a professor of history at the University of Notre Dame and Director of the Kroc Institute for International Peace Studies were the presenters. The province is pleased to offer those presentations here for continued study and reflection.

One other key player in the presentations, behind the scenes, was Pope Francis, whose style of governance in the Church reflects his own experience of religious life, and whose words of wisdom in his 2013 apostolic exhortation on the joy of the gospel, *Evangelii Gaudium*, did not fail to challenge those called to religious life. A key player behind the scenes, I say, because he is someone to whom each of the presenters made reference, someone whose insights they all valued, and someone who more than any other sees the challenges the Church faces.

Father Mascari, in terms of his previous experience as a professor at the Aquinas Institute, as Provincial, and now as an assistant with respect to the intellectual life of the Order, is in a position to see from the inside the needs and vulnerable points of the province and the Order. His theme: "The Courtyard of the Gentiles." How far out does our outreach go? Is our calling to preach primarily to the choir? Are we willing and able to move beyond our comfort zones? These are questions that his presentation raised for me. As Michael points out, the image of the courtyard of the Gentiles on the outer ring of the Temple in Jerusalem was already used by Pope Benedict, and more recently by the Master of the Order in order to help us reflect on the relationship between Dominican study and mission. We need to continue to explore the depth the image offers. It is also related to Pope Francis' exhortation: "Proclaiming the Gospel message to different cultures also involves proclaiming it to professional, scientific, and academic circles" (#132). Is this not the Dominican vocation? Michael emphasizes that we come to the courtyard first in order to listen, something that we as Dominicans do not always find easy, but he also adds, "Although we are in the Courtyard to learn, to listen, and to sit with the other, we cannot forget that we also have something to share from our study. Dominican study can never be understood merely as an academic exercise, nor as an activity that takes place in a vacuum." And he later adds: "I do not pretend that it is easy for any of us to venture into the Courtyard of the Gentiles. To be there requires intellectual honesty and humility." These thoughts only scratch the surface of what Michael has to offer which is why his text deserves a contemplative reading.

And so what do we do with respect to Dominican study? Are we ready? Prepared? If Pope Francis is someone to whom each of the presenters referred, so is his theme of evangelization. Proclaiming the gospel takes us beyond those who have already heard. Among youth, in a secular world, with the separation of reason from the life of faith, in the midst of religious pluralism, challenged by the reality of racism, as we have recently been in St. Louis, what do we have to say, and how are we to say it? What does it mean to preach in the context of our world today? I think of Dietrich Bonhoeffer's haunting challenge from his prison cell, from which he gave witness to the cost of discipleship, how to talk about God in a religionless society or secular world, especially when God is what the society so desperately needs.

Dominic saw himself as *predicationis humilis minister.* Dominic had the desire to go with William of Montferrat and preach among the

Cumans. Vincent de Couesnogle, when Master of the Order, asked the question: Who are our Cumans?[1] We now can ask, who are our Gentiles? What is the goal of our study as well as our understanding of "the preaching"?

Archbishop Tobin's questions were equally affirming, inspiring, and challenging as he addressed the topic of the role of religious in the 21st century. He too referred to both Pope Benedict and Pope Francis when talking about consecrated life and followed in particular the direction that Francis himself took in his apostolic exhortation. Consider for a moment the pastoral dimension of religious life. Are we more concerned about our personal freedom than about the gospel? Is pastoral service only an appendage to our lives rather than part of our identity? What has become of our passion for evangelization? Can the shortage of vocations be attributed to a lack of contagious apostolic fervor? These are Francis' questions. Tobin himself then unpacks a succinct statement of his about the future of religious life: "My response is that religious life will include an unmistakable witness to Jesus Christ, lived in a fraternal community and tied to missionary service on the margins or frontiers of the Church and society." The statement contains four emphases: witnessing to Jesus Christ; within a fraternal and communal reality; with a sense of mission and service; at the heart of which is a mission on the frontiers. For Dominicans none of these are new,[2] even if they need to be frequently re-appropriated.

As the archbishop points out, the primacy of God in our lives demands a deeply personal relationship with Jesus Christ that is lived radically in faith nourished by the Word of God and the liturgy. One

---

[1] Vincent de Couesnongle, *Confidence for the Future* (Dublin: Dominican Publications, 1982): 163-167. Vincent de Couesnongle was Master of the Order from 1974-1983. This compilation of his letters written while Master is still worth reading in which he addresses facing the future with courage, the power of evangelical mercy, how the young are to be received in our communities, etc. The collection of Damian Byrne's letters to the Order is likewise worth re-visiting, *A Pilgrimage of Faith* (Dominican Publications, 1991). As Master from 1983-1992 he too addressed themes such as the challenge of evangelization, the ministry of preaching, the common life, and first assignments.

[2] Take a look at the *Acta* of General Chapters going back as far as Quezon City (1977), Walberberg (1980), Rome (1983), and especially Avila (1986).

might say that this is the cornerstone for Dominicans, the *contemplari* in which our *tradere* must always be grounded, as Thomas Aquinas interpreted our way of life (*Summa Theologiae*, II-II, q 188, a 6). Tobin explores the significance of the word "witness" and prefers that we religious see ourselves as witnesses more than as prophets. Witness involves communities that are intergenerational, multicultural, and often multilingual, giving testimony to the world that harmony is possible. Tobin expressed affectionate respect for Timothy Radcliffe, Master from 1992-2001, who spoke about vocation as a mystery of love. This witness, as tied as it is both to life in common and to presence in the world (one is reminded of Lacordaire's twofold *présence à Dieu* and *présence au monde)*, must find its place at the margins or with the marginalized. Tobin writes, "I invite you to recall where a significant portion of the ministry of Jesus took place. Jesus is in a religious and social no-man's land, a place where pious Jews would not be comfortable."

As with Father Mascari, so with Archbishop Tobin, their thoughtful presentations deserve several readings. It is not a question of "been there, read that," but of reading and then pondering the words in our hearts. What more vital question to ask than who we as religious are called to be in the 21st century, and what more vital place to explore that than in the courtyard of the Gentiles, which parallels Tobin's emphasis on where Jesus himself went. We are neither to be confined nor defined by life within a cloister, and yet to see that the cloister enables one to live a life deeply grounded in God, or as Meister Eckhart would put it, in the ground of one's soul, or as St. Catherine had to learn, to walk on two feet or fly with two wings. It is both, and that is at the heart of the Dominican vocation. Dominic's own *cum Deo et de Deo* means that we must stand both in the heart and joy of the gospel and at the same time in the courtyard of the Gentiles. That is the Dominican vision; that is our challenge — simply to be faithful to our charism.

Coming more from within the courtyard of the Gentiles, as a university professor, Scott Appleby took a look at the continuing relevance of the Dominican vocation through the lens of American Catholicism, of which he is an astute student. His emphasis on the globalization of Catholicism readily connects with the two themes we have already mentioned in the two previous talks: that of ministry in the courtyard, and being there as agents of evangelization.

The same question that lay within the other two presentations is also his question: "*How are we* to meet the challenge of integrating study with service, preaching with practice, contemplation with action?" For Dominic, how could he study off dead skins when men, women and children were needlessly dying of hunger? Appleby also places the emphases of Pope Francis clearly within this Dominican spiritual tradition. Yet how does our age differ from that of Dominic's? Only ours is truly an "age of globalization." He quotes the challenge of Boston College's Lisa Sowle Cahill: the call for "a twenty-first-century Christian response to the global realities of human inequality, poverty, violence, and ecological destruction—a response that can link the power of the gospel to cross-cultural, cross-generational and interreligious cooperation for change."[3]

The world of Dominic, Albert and Thomas was also an age of globalization — the integration of the thought of Aristotle, the Jewish and Muslim interpretations of Aristotle — as well as an era calling for evangelization: "the Holy Preaching" initiated by Pope Innocent III, Bishop Diego of Osma, St. Dominic, and Bishop Foulques of Toulouse. What do evangelization and study look like in our age, the secular age, and a globalized age? Appleby asks us: Can the Dominicans meet their part of the challenge? As did Archbishop Tobin, he made particular reference to the youth, young seekers. We do not do all that needs to be done by ourselves as professed Dominicans; we educate and have an impact on others, respecting the role of the laity both in the Church and in the world. We need them as they need us. Appleby says: "Imagine a cohort of Dominican-influenced young men and women who will serve in government, in nongovernmental organizations and in the private sector, crafting alternatives to environmental degradation, militarism, exploitation of the labor force, government inefficiency and corruption, and other pressing, globalized social, economic and political challenges. Ensuring the 'Dominican influence' is a formidable task, I realize, but it is one commensurate with your history, mission and charism."

---

[3] Lisa Sowle Cahill, *Global Justice, Christology and Christian Ethics*, New Studies in Christian Ethics (Cambridge: Cambridge University Press, 2013).

As we look back at the past seventy-five years of the province, and ahead to the next seventy-five, and to those who have gone before us carrying the torch, and to those who will continue carrying the torch in the decades ahead, Mascari, Tobin, and Appleby have set the bar high for us: Are we up for the challenge? Can we truly be contemplative in the midst of our world? Does our learning have something to contribute in the courtyard of the Gentiles? What will become of our witness?

This past autumn I was fortunate to have the opportunity to spend forty days in a hermitage on the property of the Sisters of Charity in Nazareth, Kentucky, within a half hour of St. Rose and St. Catharine's, where the Dominican Family had its start in this "new world." It must have seemed to them as well like a globalized world and new era for evangelization. The Sisters of Charity came to that area in 1812 and to Nazareth in 1822. During my daily walks amid autumn leaves, roaming deer, and wild turkeys, I would pass through the cemetery on the motherhouse property usually twice a day — where close to 2000 sisters have been buried. The oldest tombstone I found was dated 1818. It was a powerful experience to walk through one's cemetery, to see those who have gone before us, to read our history in those graves, to know that we will ourselves someday be there, and our names read during the "De Profundis." One then can indeed see that we are part of a picture bigger than ourselves, that others before us have faithfully and courageously carried the torch, a torch that always gets passed on to a new generation.

We say thank you once again for all that has been, and yes once again to what is to come. The challenge is simple and yet profound: the torch must go on in an ever more and more complex world. That is our challenge. That is the grace. But it is our conviction that the Holy Spirit does not let one down, nor does the one to whom our Order had been entrusted, the Blessed Mother, let down those who have recourse to her.

Religious in the Church of the 21st Century

Archbishop Joseph Tobin, C.Ss.R.

Introduction

When I used to work honestly in the Church, I was the pastor of a parish served by the Redemptorists on the North Side of Chicago. Though I was sent to Rome from there more twenty-three years ago, some of the parishioners still stay in touch. Just after Easter last year I received an email from Tom, a young father in that neighborhood. I had baptized his son, Sam, and Tom told me about a conversation the two of them had one Sunday, walking home from mass.

It seems that the Dad was struggling a bit to understand the homily they had heard. He turned to Sam, a bright seven-year-old—who was preparing to receive his first Holy Communion and thus paying attention to <u>everything</u> that happened in church—and asked, "Sam, to whom do you think Father was talking this morning: to the kids or to the grown-ups?"

Sam pondered the problem, then confidently affirmed, "I think he was talking to himself!"

Talking to oneself is an occupational hazard for preachers, at least for Redemptorists! Some of the People of God maintain that our abbreviation, "C.Ss.R.," stands for "**C**arefully **S**elected **S**ermons, **R**epeated". I am sure that the Order of Preachers never merit such damning critique.

I am also confident that today I will not be talking to myself, since I have been invited to reflect on a theme that interests us all: the role of religious life in the Church of the 21st century. Over the course of the eighteen years that I served on the General Council of my religious family, I made a lot of visitations; we Redemptorists work in seventy-eight countries and I spent about half of each of those years on the road. During the initial meeting with the local community, I tried to be clear with the brethren why I was there. I said that I hadn't come as a cop; nor was I there as a tourist. Rather, like them, I had bet the most precious of my possessions – my life – on the proposition of following Jesus Christ in the charism of my Congregation. I suggested to the brethren that we discuss the wager that we had made in the hope of living that option more authentically.

So I am grateful to Father Bouchard and the brothers of the Province of St. Albert the Great for this opportunity to speak about the option we all have made, the wager, if you will, of our very lives. Here is what I intend to do. First, I would like to frame the question of consecrated life in the new millennium by contrasting some critical views regarding its present predicament and its future, paying special attention to the opinion of our Holy Father, Pope Francis. I hope that the context will allow me to present some thoughts about the place of consecrated life and its testimony in the Church. Finally, I will offer some suggestions regarding our witness in the particular circumstances of the United States.

You will soon be able to judge whether I have anything terribly interesting to say about consecrated life. What gives me confidence to share these thoughts with you is the wisdom of my paternal grandmother, who hailed from a renowned corner of Ireland called Glencar, Co. Kerry. During my misspent youth, she would look at me with great sympathy and observe, "Joseph, each one of us is useful for something, even as a bad example."

The State of the Question: Three categories of lies

In my opinion, at the present moment of the pilgrimage, an essential question for the holiness and wholeness of consecrated people demands that we look at our place in the Church. How does our vocation relate to other particular vocations in the communion of the Church, especially those of her Pastors and laity? What is helpful for our understanding, of course, is to glimpse how these other vocations understand ours. A sample interpretation given to the phenomena of diminishing numbers of religious may help to illustrate my point.

Mark Twain designated statistics as one of the three categories of lies ("lies, damned lies and statistics") because their interpretation can be anything but scientific. Let us begin with an unquestionable fact:

there has been a steady decline in the number of consecrated men and women in Western Europe, Australia and New Zealand, as well as North America in the last five decades. Even in Eastern Europe, which had enjoyed an impressive surge in numbers after the fall of the Berlin Wall, as well as in some Latin American countries, there are worrisome indicators that suggest the wave has crested and the tide may be going out.

Like religious, the Pastors of the Church have tried to understand the reason for such a precipitous decline. Many bishops conclude that religious have discarded some essential elements of their vocation. This way of thinking was expressed with unusual frankness in an article that appeared in L'Osservatore Romano shortly after I began to work for the Holy See in late August 2010. The author, himself a religious who was serving as Secretary in another dicastery of the Roman Curia, severely criticized religious for being agents of "self-secularization". He stated that, as a result of decisions made to abandon the habit, traditional residences and apostolic works, **practically all of the active congregations born in the nineteenth or early twentieth century now find themselves to be mortally wounded and their disappearance is simply a question of time** [the translation and emphasis are mine].[4]

At the time of their *ad limina* visits, bishops came to my former workplace (the dicastery charged with accompanying consecrated life across the world) and frequently expressed concern over the declining numbers of consecrated men and women in their respective dioceses. This was especially true when the American bishops made their *ad limina* visits in 2011-12. What is lost as a charismatic presence wanes in a particular Church? Most often, the Pastors were saddened by the withdrawal of religious from projects that had produced abundant good in their jurisdictions, such as pastoral service in parishes, oratories and sanctuaries, as well as the management of schools,

---

[4] S. E. R. Jean-Louis Bruguès, OP, "Riscoprire l'essenziale della vocazione per sottrarsi ai condizionamenti della società: Vita religiosa e secolarizzazione", *L'Osservatore Romano*, 20 October 2010. The original text of the statement is: "la quasi totalità delle congregazioni attive, nate nel XIX o all'inizio del XX, si trovano quindi colpite a morte, e la loro scomparsa è solo una questione di tempo".

hospitals, residences for the aged or those with special needs, etc.

Pope Benedict XVI

For his part, Pope Benedict XVI had a different notion about the place of consecrated people in the Church and what their absence might mean for a diocese. After assuming the Petrine service in 2005, the Holy Father expressed openly his gratitude for consecrated life as well as his judgment that our vocation forms an integral part of the mission of the Church. An example of his thinking can be found in a discourse he offered to a group of Brazilian bishops, who made their visit *ad limina* in late 2010.[5] On that occasion, the Holy Father called consecrated life "a select portion of the People of God"[6] and, using an image borrowed from his predecessor, he compared consecrated life to "a plant with many branches which sinks its roots into the Gospel and brings forth abundant fruit in every season of the Church's life."[7] Since love is the greatest of the charismatic gifts, a religious community enriches a particular Church, first and foremost, with its witness to love.

Far from foreseeing its inevitable disappearance, Pope Benedict taught that consecrated life began with the Lord, who chose for himself a life that is virginal, poor and obedient. Hence, consecrated life can never leave the Church or die, since Jesus intended it to be a permanent feature of his Church.[8] Therefore, the whole Church is obliged to promote vocations to the consecrated life.

I would mention in passing that in the first year of his pontificate, Benedict XVI held an assembly in which he spoke to all the superiors general of women's and men's institutes who were resident in Roma.

---

[5] *Discurso do Papa Bento XV aos Prelados da Conferencia Nacional dos Bispos do Brasil (Regional Sul II) em visita «ad limina apostolorum», quinta-feira, 5 de novembro de 2010.*
[6] Literally "porção eleita do Povo de Deus", ibid.
[7] The Pope cites n. 5 of the apostolic exhortation *Vita Consecrata* (25 March 1996).
[8] "mas a vida consagrada como tal teve origem com o próprio Senhor que escolheu para Si esta forma de vida virgem, pobre e obediente. Por isso a vida consagrada nunca poderá faltar nem morrer na Igreja: foi querida pelo próprio Jesus como parcela irremovível da sua Igreja."; ibid.

More significantly, in February 2008, he granted a lengthy private audience to the leadership of the two Unions of superiors general – an extraordinary event that had not happened for over twenty years.

A word from a friend

And now the members of consecrated life clearly have a great friend named Francis. The first member of the Society of Jesus to be elected pope, Francis is also the first religious since the election in 1831of the Camaldolese monk, Mauro Cappellari, who chose the name Gregory XVI.

Francis has not downplayed his identity as a Jesuit nor has he avoided meeting the leadership of religious life. On June 6, 2013, the Pope received the board of the CLAR (la *Confederación Latinoamericana y Caribeña de Religiosos y Religiosas*, the Latin American and Caribbean Confederation of Religious Men and Women). According to a purported transcript of the meeting[9], Pope Francis treated themes that, in fact, would later appear in his apostolic exhortation, *Evangelii Gaudium*, [10] such as the need for the Church to live the Gospel more courageously, even at the risk of making mistakes, as well as some illustrations that would eventually appear in the apostolic exhortation, such as the scandalous contrast between the death of a street person, which engenders little interest, and the chaos caused by the slightest downturn in the stock market. Francis reportedly told the Latin American religious to "open doors, do something where life is calling you."

Last November 29th Francis held an extensive dialogue with members of the Union of Superiors General (USG), the association of the general superiors of institutes of men.[11] The Holy Father welcomed

---

[9] The transcript of the June 6th meeting was first published by the website of Reflexión y Liberación http://www.reflexionyliberacion.cl/articulo/2729/papa-francisco-dialoga-como-un-hermano-mas-con-la-clar.html) and later translated into English by another website, Rorate Coeli (http://rorate-caeli.blogspot.com/2013/06/pope-to-latin-american-religious-full.html)

[10] Francis, post-synodal apostolic exhortation Evangelii Gaudium, (November 24, 2014); henceforward EG.

[11] A summary of the meeting was published by *La Civiltà Cattolica*, which

questions, spoke of his experience as a major superior and a bishop and offered an enthusiastic invitation to religious to "wake up the world!"

Five days prior to that meeting, Francis published his first great programmatic statement, the apostolic exhortation *Evangelii Gaudium*, "The Joy of the Gospel," which completed the work of the XIII Ordinary General Assembly of the Synod of Bishops concerning the so-called "New Evangelization." I hope you have had the opportunity to study this stimulating text. Perhaps, like me, you were struck by the three explicit references that Pope Francis makes to consecrated life. These citations apparently never came up in his meeting with the USG. Maybe the generals had not yet had time to read the text; perhaps the Holy Father's critique was clear and indisputable.

The three references occur in the second chapter of the exhortation, the portion of the document in which Pope Francis wishes "to mention briefly the context in which we all have to live and work."[12] After discussing some of the challenges posed by a globalized world, he turns to some particular temptations that are faced by pastoral workers. It is here that he refers explicitly to our way of life.

First, he speaks about pastoral agents, "including consecrated men and women," who display "an inordinate concern for their personal freedom and relaxation" that leads them to consider pastoral service as a "mere appendage to their life", not part of their very identity.[13] The spiritual life comes to be identified with "a few religious exercises" without "encouraging a real encounter with others, engagement with the world or a passion for evangelization."[14] The Holy Father points out that such pastoral agents may in fact pray but nevertheless exhibit "a heightened individualism, a crisis of identity and a cooling of fervour" three evils that, in his view, fuel one another.[15]

Turning from the temptations faced by individuals, the Holy Father

---

offers an English translation on its website (http://www.laciviltacattolica.it/articoli_download/extra/Wake_up_the_world.pdf)

[12] *EG* 50
[13] *EG* 78
[14] Ibid.
[15] Ibid.

invites us to recognize the painful fact that some Christian communities "and even consecrated persons" are tolerant of different forms of enmity, division, calumny, defamation, vendetta, jealous and the "desire to impose certain ideas at all costs, even to persecutions which appear as veritable witch hunts."[16] Such internal strife cannot help but vitiate any efforts at evangelization.

Finally, Pope Francis examines the shortage of vocations to the priesthood and religious life that, in many cases, can be attributed to "a lack of contagious apostolic fervour in communities, which results in a cooling of enthusiasm and attractiveness."[17] The Holy Father is confident that "wherever there is life, fervour and a desire to bring Christ to others, genuine vocations will arise."[18]

Pope Francis avoids what, in my mind, is an unhelpful dichotomy that has hamstrung discussions about religious life: a distinction between "being" and "doing", as if one could simply *be* a religious and call into question one's way of living. The Holy Father's critique of religious life is rooted in his antipathy towards a whole set of behaviors that he groups under the classical vice of *acedia*, which he describes as a "state of paralysis" caused by a number of factors, including a shallow or superficial assessment of one's capabilities, leading to unrealistic commitments, impatience, a slothful passivism and an intolerance for "anything that smacks of disagreement, possible failure, criticism, the cross."[19] *Acedia* is the polar opposite of the central value of the apostolic exhortation and, one might argue, the axial value of Francis's self-understanding: the joy of the Gospel.

We should take seriously these criticisms, since the Gospel is the "ultimate norm" and to be considered the "highest rule" of religious life,[20] and any attitudes that lead us away from a joyful appropriation and proclamation of the Gospel must be challenged. As one who has tried to live the vowed life for more than forty years, having spent nearly thirty of those in the service of government, I accept Francis's

---

[16] *EG* 100
[17] *EG* 107
[18] Ibid.
[19] cf. *EG* 81-82.
[20] Second Vatican Council, Decree on the Adaptation and Renewal of Religious Life *Perfectae Caritatis*, (October 28, 1965), 2.

criticism as timely and accurate.

But, like the folks who were "cut to the heart" by Peter's discourse on the first Pentecost, we might turn to Francis and ask "Brother, what are we to do?" (cf. Acts 2, 38). By inviting me to the assembly, you posed that question to me. My response is that religious life will include an unmistakable witness to Jesus Christ, lived in a fraternal community and tied to missionary service on the margins or frontiers of the Church and society. Let me explain these three challenges, which I believe will be the characteristics of a future flourishing of religious life.

What are we to do? We are his witnesses...

In one of his seminal works on spirituality, *The Practice of the Love of Jesus Christ*, St. Alphonsus tells the story of a hermit who one day met a prince in the forest. The prince asked him what he was doing there. The hermit replies by asking the prince, "Sir, what are you doing in this lonely place?" When the prince answered that he was hunting wild animals, the hermit responded, "And I am hunting for God," and went on his way.[21] If it is true that many of our contemporaries are searching for the divine or, at least, for some ultimate meaning in their lives, imagine the powerful witness of religious life as the "place" where men and women are hunting for God!

Religious life was born as an affirmation of the absolute claim of God on human beings and, as historians point out, first appeared at the time in history when martyrdom ceased to be a feature of Christian communities, leading to a diminishing appreciation for the radical character of the Gospel. Thus, an affirmation of the primacy of God, the One who is to be loved with an undivided heart, represents the first and most essential quality of the consecrated life. God is the One who gives reason to and motivation for the conduct of consecrated men and women.

There is a danger that, because of their dedication to pastoral activity or works of service, consecrated persons inordinately sacrifice

---

[21] Pratica dell'Amore di Gesù Cristo, II, 8.

their witness to a radically Christian life, that is, to the effort towards being, first and foremost, seekers of God and true Christians. Without such a struggle, there cannot be a true consecrated life. Without this dimension that touches on the *being* of consecrated people, all their activity can lose its fundamental *raison d'être*.

This truth was brought home to me during my first years of ministry. I was part of a community serving a large, poor parish in the inner city of Detroit. We made every effort to ensure that the parish responded to the needs of the neighborhood, a point of arrival for thousands of immigrants from the whole of Latin America. I recall one afternoon sitting in a rectory parlor, listening to a young Mexican mother extol the virtues of our parish. She said that she could do practically everything there: vaccinate her children, learn English, regularize her status with the immigration laws, send her children to school. However, with great simplicity she added that whenever she wanted to pray, she went to another church. I was shocked to realize that, while we were providing a vast array of services, our testimony was disconnected from the "one thing necessary" (cf. Lk 10, 41-42).

The primacy of God above all demands that religious:

a) live *a deeply personal relationship with Jesus Christ*: the consecrated person needs to be in love with Christ; religious life is above all a "passion for Christ", a fascination with His person and His way of life. For this reason, I prefer that we call ourselves "witnesses" rather than prophets. The apostles identified themselves as "witnesses" of the saving action God in Jesus Christ and dare to associate the Holy Spirit with their testimony (Acts 5, 32). I do not find the apostles – or anyone else in either Testament – calling themselves "prophets". Rather, other people come to judge certain words and actions as prophetic, that is, as testimony to God the Father and our Lord Jesus Christ.

While admitting that Pope Francis recently called on the general superiors "follow the Lord in a prophetic way,"[22] there

---

[22] cf. summary of his meeting with the USG on November 29, 2013; note 8 above.

are two reasons why I prefer that we religious live as "his witnesses" rather than prophets. First, witness – especially *his* witnesses – maintains the fundamentally Christocentric nature of religious life. Secondly, in some of the polemic that has emerged from conflicts between religious and Pastors, the misuse of the word "prophetic" has led to an exaggerated juxtaposition between religious life and the structures of the Church, which, thirty-five years ago, the instruction *Mutuae Relationes* already saw as a "serious error", capable of deluding Pastors and religious into thinking and acting "as if they could subsist as two distant entities, one charismatic, the other institutional." Citing the doctrine of *Lumen Gentium*, the instructions reminds us that both elements, namely the spiritual gifts and the ecclesial structures "form *one*, even though *complex reality*" (cf. *LG* 8)."[23]

b) live *radically in faith*: the choice for consecrated life is a confident and demanding profession of faith in God. The Church asks consecrated persons and their communities to cultivate seriously such faith and become models who are not content with simply following the external manifestations of religiosity. Before anything else, consecrated people should be in the Church "specialists in faith", while, at the same time, knowing how to wisely accompany believers who are look for a more demanding way to live their faith.

c) nurture their witness by drawing on *the authentic sources for a spiritual life* (a forceful demand of the Second Vatican Council), namely the *Word of God* and the *Liturgy*. Here again consecrated people are expected to be examples, demonstrating to all that their spiritual life is nourished regularly and substantially by the Word and the Liturgy instead of a steady diet of devotional practices or even, in some parts of the Church, esoteric "revelations"...

When speaking of consecrated life as radical witness, it is useful to

---

[23] Sacred Congregation for Religious and Secular Institutes; Sacred *Congregation for Bishops, Directives for the Mutual Relations between Bishops and Religious in the Church* (hereafter, MR), Roma: 14 May 1978; 34.

underscore yet again a problem that afflicts religious in many countries, including our own: a marked decrease in numbers and their advancing age, together with some unavoidable consequences. Even this particular situation is an invitation for religious to live with an attitude of faith. A beautiful text of the apostolic exhortation *Vita consecrata* can inspire us:

> The various difficulties stemming from the decline in personnel and apostolates *must in no way lead to a loss of confidence in the evangelical vitality of the consecrated life*, which will always be present and active in the Church. (...) New situations of difficulty are therefore to be faced with the serenity of those who know that what is required of each individual is *not success, but commitment to faithfulness*. What must be avoided at all costs is the actual breakdown of the consecrated life, a collapse which is not measured by a decrease in numbers but by a failure to cling steadfastly to the Lord and to one's personal vocation and mission.[24]

A Gospel based fraternity

Much has been written about fraternal life as a constituent element of religious life. I would like to propose two ways that fraternal life might respond to the "signs of times and places" in the contemporary circumstances of the United States.

A thoughtful reading of the account of Pentecost (Acts 1,1-13) suggests that the event features at least two miracles. First, a kaleidoscope of cultures hear the Good News "each...in his own native language" (1, 8). The second miracle is more subtle but nonetheless spectacular: after they hear the Good News and ask for baptism, there is no evidence that the listeners cease being "Parthians, Medes, and Elamites, inhabitants of Mesopotamia, Judea and Cappadocia, Pontus and Asia, Phrygia and Pamphylia, Egypt and the districts of Libya near Cyrene, as well as travelers from Rome." The Gospel does not require

---

[24] Vita Consecrata, 63.

them to sacrifice their culture and, though the first disputes in the community suggest uneasy relations between ethnic groups,[25] the miracle is the determination of the community to go to any length to prevent a rupture. We can trace these wonders to the work of the Holy Spirit, who leads the community to truth (cf. John 16, 13) and gives the members the determination and power to overcome what divides them.

In some parts of this country today international Institutes of consecrated life privilege the witness of multicultural communities of Brothers and Sisters. These communities have the potential of realizing a prophetic testimony that was described by Blessed John Paul II in *Vita Consecrata*:

> The Church entrusts to communities of consecrated life the particular task of spreading the spirituality of communion, first of all in their internal life and then in the ecclesial community, and even beyond its boundaries, by opening or continuing a dialogue in charity, especially where today's world is torn apart by ethnic hatred or senseless violence. Placed as they are within the world's different societies — societies frequently marked by conflicting passions and interests, seeking unity but uncertain about the ways to attain it — communities of consecrated life, where persons of different ages, languages and cultures meet as brothers and sisters, are signs that dialogue is always possible and that communion can bring differences into harmony.
>
> (...) In an age characterized by the globalization of problems and the return of the idols of nationalism, international Institutes especially are called to uphold and to bear witness to the sense of communion between peoples, races and cultures. (...) International Institutes can achieve this effectively, inasmuch as they

---

[25] Such as the clash between Greek and Hebrew speakers (6, 1-6) and the more serious dispute over circumcision, which culminated in the so-called "Council of Jerusalem" (Acts 15, 1ff.).

have to face in a creative way the challenge of inculturation, while at the same time preserving their identity.[26]

I believe that consecrated life in the United States is called today to offer a particular witness to brother- and sisterhood by creating communities in which persons of different ages, languages and cultures meet in fraternity and become "signs that dialogue is always possible and that communion can bring differences into harmony".

Such communities do not happen by accident. Throwing together in the same community Brothers or Sisters from a variety of cultural backgrounds and then hoping for the best is a recipe for disaster. There is a need to inculturate the community, but also to root the members in the culture of the Institute. I believe that this is what John Paul II is calling for when he asks international institutes to face creatively the challenge of inculturation while at the same time preserving their identity.

In years past, while visiting my confreres in Siberia, I admired the communities that had been established by the Order of Friars Minor in different parts of the Russian Republic. Among the reasons that motivated the Order to form multicultural communities in Russia was an effort to lessen the possibility that Catholic Christianity would be narrowly identified with a single nation, possibly raising the suspicions of the inhabitants or the dominant form of Christianity. It is instructive to know how the Franciscans began these communities.

The Friars explained to me that the first members of the new communities went to Assisi where, with the assistance of one of the General Definitors, the missionaries reflected on the charism of their Order as a gift to the people of Russia. More precisely, they tried to imagine what it would mean to offer a witness to fraternity by means of international communities implanted in regions where the Catholic Church had a fragile presence and no real institutions. My impression was that this period of preparation served well the new mission.

It would be a great gift to the Church and consecrated life, if

---

[26] *Vita Consecrata*, 51

Institutes in the United States would commit themselves to forming multicultural communities, which had a thoughtful and holistic preparation, including the development of the necessary strategies to deal with the sort of conflict that can occur when religious of different cultures live and minister together. It seems to me that another element of this formation would be an effort to enhance the particular "culture" of the Institute – values, rituals, prayer and other elements that identify the Institute in the different countries in which it is present.

In a nation that often reacts fearfully to the presence of the other and is reinforcing barriers to keep out migrants and refugees, the witness of multicultural communities of consecrated people can be a powerful witness to God, who "shows no partiality" (Acts 10, 34).

Ethnic diversity is not the sole source of cultural pluralism within the Church or religious life. A problem for consecrated life in the United States may be that we are slow to recognize the religious aspirations of young people today. Let me try to illustrate this with two examples, admittedly taken from the experience of other countries. Some years ago I was speaking with Timothy Radcliffe, then Master General of the Dominicans, about the situation of his Order in France. Timothy astounded me by saying that the Dominicans then had forty-five or so professed students in that country. He added that the Toulouse province featured an average age of forty-seven, if my memory serves me right.

Once I saw that Timothy was not joking – I had the impression that there were not forty-five men in formation among all the orders and dioceses in France – I asked him to explain the Dominicans' apparent success. He reminded me that vocation is always a mystery of love, which resists analysis solely in demographic terms, but he did suggest that there were two critical elements behind the flourishing. First, the Order had made concrete decisions to clarify its identity in France. Secondly, as Master of the Order, Timothy had to intervene between the young professed and confreres from the so-called generation of *soixante-huit*, the grizzled veterans of the enthusiasm and upheaval of the 1960's. Otherwise, the older confreres would eat these young alive, judging that their appreciation for habits, regular order and common prayer was simply a reactionary fantasy that would result in the Order reassuming the "chains" that had been justly discarded decades before.

I have found a similar logic in units of my own Congregation. I remember taking part in a provincial chapter in Australia five or six years ago. The province had received one or two professions in the last fifteen years. When I asked about candidates, a number of capitulars agreed in quite dismissive terms that the only type of inquirers the province was receiving were so-called "right-wing kids". I suggested that they might call the young people "different" and wondered whether we were able to afford a new generation the same privilege that the baby-boomers claimed: that of being distinct from our elders.

In a society that is Balkanized by generational differences, communities of religious can provide an alternative example of unity as a mutual exchange of gifts.

Mission on the margins and frontiers

After spending more than two decades outside of the United States, I try to understand what has changed and why. I have described elsewhere three relatively new narratives that appear to dominate an understanding of the predicament of consecrated life in this country.[27] Individually, the stories of the sexual abuse crisis, diminishment and aging, and a culture that esteems professionalism, are all rooted in reality and in this sense are true. My question is whether these powerful stories have not deafened the members of our orders and congregations to other possibilities. We might think of ourselves as Elijah, cowering in the cave on Mount Horeb (1 Kings 19, 5-13). The deafening blasts and crushing force of these narratives threaten us, suck away our hope and keep us in the security of our caves. Amid this unnerving cacophony, is there also a "tiny, whispering sound" that might draw us out of our hidey-hole?

In suggesting an answer, I invite you to recall where that a significant portion of the ministry of Jesus took place. Jesus is in a religious and social no-man's land, a place where pious Jews would not

---

[27] See, for example, my address to the annual assembly of the Conference of Major Superiors of Men (August 2010), later published in *Origens*.

be comfortable. Some of the pericopes suggest that Jesus himself probably had to be convinced that his mission was to people in these places as well as to the house of Israel. I am convinced that God is calling the consecrated to witness to God and God's kingdom in a similar "place" today.

This "place" is being dramatically created, even expanded, through a process of "boundary maintenance" in both society and the Church. Émile Durkheim proposed that law and crime function to mark the boundaries of acceptable and unacceptable behaviour in any large-scale society. That is, they represent broad social guidelines for people's behavior. As historians know, boundaries, be they cultural, ethical or geographic, can be revised. This is not necessarily a bad thing. I think that the Council of Jerusalem (Acts 15), the Nicene Creed and the doctrine of Vatican II are all represent some sort of boundary maintenance, insofar as they are efforts to clarify the identity of a group by elucidating its essential norms.

I believe we can agree that both society and Church are engaged in a process of boundary maintenance. In part, this movement has been provoked by postmodernity — understood as a set of cultural circumstances that signifies the "obliteration of boundaries and the confusion of categories".[28] Societies experience globalization and the mass migration of peoples; the Church wrestles with relativism and a vapid catechesis. As a result, new lines are drawn in the sands of the Sonoran Desert, while clear doctrinal statements seem to short-circuit dialogue.

Fresh or reinforced boundaries create new spaces in which the marginalized are consigned. In apparent contradiction of the norms and cultural practices of the Judaism of his time, Jesus heals the deaf man, cures a hemorrhaging woman and feeds a multitude in pagan territory, a place that could not be seen from the heights of Jerusalem. But this "space" existed also within the traditional territory of Judah. Otherwise, how can we understand the consistent accusation that was leveled against Jesus, a charge that probably led to his death: that he shared table fellowship with those beyond the pale? "Why does he eat

---

[28] John Milbank, *Being Reconciled: Ontology and Pardon*, London: Routledge, 2003, p. 187.

with tax collectors and sinners?" (Mark 2, 16).

It is easy for the Church to overlook this action of Jesus. I was a member of the 2005 Synod of Bishops that was concerned with the Eucharist. The synod lasted nearly a month and you might imagine the number of speeches that were shared and the vast range of Scripture that was reviewed. To my shame, it was only afterwards that I realized that in no debate was reference made to any verse that spoke of Jesus sharing table fellowship with sinners. Before pointing the finger at other member of that synod, I accuse myself of a scandalously bad memory.

I think that Pope Francis is aware of the space that has been created by boundary maintenance in the Church and has thought a great deal about how to reach those who feel themselves excluded. Hence, he is repeating his predecessor's consistent call to the Church that the Gospel not be presented, first and foremost, as a moral code to be obeyed, but rather as an invitation to transformation through an intimate friendship with the living God.[29]

The "place" for consecrated people today is the space where people are excluded from their full dignity as sons and daughters of God, who have been redeemed by Jesus Christ and sanctified by the Holy Spirit. This possibility is the "tiny, whispering sound" that urges us to leave the cave of our securities, be they material goods, social esteem, comfortable prejudices or cultivated cynicism. The dominant narratives of the sexual abuse crisis, the aging of our members or the demands of professionalism can easily conceal this persistent call. But, if we hear it, then we will know where God is waiting for us.

If we obey, we do not go to the marginalized and excluded in order to create some sort of parallel Church. Rather, we are willing to live with an often painful, but potentially creative tension with the Pastors, who also must recognize that the consecrated life, if it is to be true to itself, will always be a little problematic for the Shepherds. Even if we arrive first at the tomb, we are ready to step aside, so that Peter might enter. (cf. John 20, 3-8). In this way, we all come to recognize the Lord in the place of ultimate exclusion, that is, death. Together we see and

---

[29] cf, for example, the encyclical *Deus Caritas Est* (December 25, 2005), n. 14

we believe.

Conclusion

I would like to conclude this reflection with some thoughts about the first Christian community in Europe. The arrival of Paul and his companions at Philippi may offer some insight into the future of consecrated life on this continent as well.

According to Acts 16, 9-40, Paul established at Philippi the first Christian community in Europe. He came to Philippi, via its harbor town of Neapolis (the modern Kavalla), on his second missionary journey, probably in A.D. 49 or 50, accompanied by Silas and Timothy (Acts 15, 40; 16, 3; cf. Phil 1, 1) and, perhaps, Luke.[30] The Acts account tells of the conversion of a businesswoman, Lydia; the exorcism of a slave girl; and, after an earthquake, while Paul and Silas were imprisoned in Philippi, the gift of faith and baptism of a jailer and his family.[31] Acts 16 concludes its account by describing how Paul (and Silas), asked by the magistrates to leave Philippi, went on to Thessalonica (Acts 17:1-10), where several times his loyal Philippians continued to support him with financial aid (Phil 4:16). Later, Paul may have passed through Philippi on his way from Ephesus to Greece (Acts 20:1-2), and he definitely stopped there on his fateful trip to Jerusalem (Acts 20:6).

Why did Paul decide to enter Europe? Do you recall a puzzling feature in the account from Acts? The writer reports that "Holy Spirit" and "the spirit of Jesus" prevented Paul and his companions from going where they originally had intended to preach. Frustrated twice, Paul then has a dream of someone in Macedonian dress who begs him to come and help his people.

In an address to a mission agency of the Church of England, Rowan Williams, the archbishop of Canterbury, referred to this passage from Acts and spoke about the need for the Church to discern well where it

---

[30] If Luke is to be included in the "we" references of Acts 16:10-17.
[31] None of these persons, however, is directly mentioned in the Letter to the Philippians.

is called to announce the Gospel today:

> I have a sense that the Holy Spirit is saying to Paul and his companions, don't waste your energy where God at this moment is not opening a door. Keep your eyes and ears open for the door God is opening; the place where God has already in some way turned over the soil. Where do we start? Where God has started. How do we start? By listening, looking, discerning for the way in which God has turned over the soil for us.[32]

The *Lineamenta* for the 2012 Synod of Bishops on new evangelization referred twenty-four different times to the need for discernment. Recalling the experience of the primitive Church, the *Lineamenta* observed

> The process of evangelization became a process of discernment. Proclamation first requires moments of listening, understanding and interpretation.[33]

The Church is aware that the world has changed and continues to present new socio-cultural forms. A clear comparison can be made between the situation that confronted Paul and the present challenges. Tired, prefabricated solutions for the problem of evangelization no longer are acceptable. Instead, the Church must "listen, understand and interpret" before it speaks.

There is another conclusion that might be drawn from the circumstances that led Paul to Europe. In the long run, not every failed project is necessarily a defeat. What we initially judge in negative terms could actually be the work of the Holy Spirit, who impedes human projects in order to further the proclamation of the Gospel. This possibility invites us to look again at the present crisis and discern whether God may not be opening a door for the Church and, within it, the members of consecrated life.

---

[32] Rowan Williams, "God's Mission and Ours in the 21st century" (June 9, 2009), http://www.archbishopofcanterbury.org/articles.php/779/gods-mission-and-ours-in-the-21st-century .
[33] *Lineamenta*, 3.

We can also believe that personal success of the disciple is not the most important indicator of the progress of the Gospel. The church at Philippi will eventually become a sufficiently flourishing community for Paul to honor it with one of his letters. Judging from the sixteenth chapter in Acts, however, Paul's personal success was minimal. Evidently the community grew considerably after his departure and, as is clear from Paul's letter to them, he reserved his greatest affection for the Christians of Philippi.

This assembly marks the 75th anniversary of the foundation of the Province of St. Albert the Great. I understand that you will evaluate the missionary direction of your unit of the Order. I pray that this analysis might also be a moment of discernment that allows you to hear the "tiny whispering sound" of the Spirit, inviting to you to bring the gift of your charism to the margins and frontiers of Church and society.

+ Joseph W. Tobin, C.Ss.R.
Archbishop of Indianapolis

A Dominican Vision of Study: Into the Courtyard of the Gentiles

Michael Mascari, O.P.

As budding scripture scholars, our student brothers could no doubt describe the Temple of Jerusalem better than I can. Although this building complex in the time of Jesus was a pale imitation of the splendor of Solomon's temple, it nevertheless received a major face-lift in the time of Herod the Great. It was here that Jesus came from the time he was a boy, it was here that he prayed and identified himself as a member of the community of Israel, and it was here that he preached and healed and proclaimed a temple not made by human hands. The temple, which stood on what we today call the Temple Mount, consisted of a series of courtyards, most of which were concentric. In the innermost courtyard stood the Holy of Holies, where the High Priest entered only one day a year. Adjacent to it was the Sanctuary and the Court of the Priests, forbidden to all but those who were born of the tribe of Levi. Surrounding the Court of Priests, where the daily sacrifices were offered, was the Court of Men, restricted to male Jews only, and surrounding this, and therefore more distant from the court of Priests and the Holy of Holies, was the Court of Women, limited to Jewish women only.

Beyond these privileged circles that were accessible only to Jews, lay the vast courtyard of the Gentiles, open to anyone, to men and to women, to Jews and Greeks, to those who believed in the God of Israel and to those who did not, to those who were learned in the Law and to those who had come with questions, to those who had come to worship and to those who had come to conduct business, a place where priests, pious Jews, Roman soldiers, moneychangers, teachers with their students, and not yet circumcised proselytes mingled freely, where the smell of incense, the glitter of coins, and the bleating of goats and sheep added to the sights and smells of a marketplace. The Court of the Gentiles was a space that was safe and secure, where all kinds of exchange took place, where one could haggle over a price, argue and debate a position, or gather around a rabbi to learn and to ask questions, a forum where a person was free to express what he thought and what he believed.

In an address to the Roman Curia on 21 December 2009, Pope Benedict XVI called to mind this Court of the Gentiles, so evocative of a Middle-Eastern bazaar, as a way for the Church to think about its mission. Speaking of the need to reach atheists, agnostics, and others who were seeking an experience of transcendence, Benedict encouraged the Church to "open a kind of 'Court of the Gentiles' in which people might in some way latch on to God, without consciously knowing him and before gaining access to the mystery of God, at whose service the inner life of the Church stands."

In his own thinking and in his writing, the Master of the Order has used this image of the Courtyard of the Gentiles to help us reflect upon the mission of the Order, including our understanding of study. For example, he has challenged the institutions under his immediate jurisdiction to move beyond their areas of expertise and to engage those whose views of God, society, nature, and political life are quite different from our own. In provinces where the intellectual life is quite specialized and perhaps even narrow, he has invited the brothers to consider a different path for pursuing research and for contributing to the intellectual life of their region.

In places where the churches are full each week with strong, committed Catholics, he has wondered whether this might not be the time to give such parishes back to the diocese so that our brothers can address those who have not heard the Gospel or who have become marginalized and grown distant from the Church. Always he asks the Order, "who is missing? Who is not here? Who has been left out? Whose ideas are not being heard, whose perspectives are not being taken into account, whose longings are not being addressed when we preach and when we teach?" He is concerned that as Dominicans we sometimes insulate ourselves and surround ourselves with like-minded believers, people who look at the church and the world in the way that we do. Too often we position ourselves squarely and securely within the inner sanctuary of the Temple, afraid to venture out and to enter into the messy world of those around us.

Like Pope Benedict and the Master, I think this image of the Courtyard of the Gentiles is one that we also can reflect upon fruitfully in our own consideration of study. Last summer, in his letter to the Province for the Feast of St. Dominic our provincial presented what I believe is an insightful picture of our province. It is a province of wide-open spaces, with brothers who are consensus-oriented, collaborative in their manner, who like to question, who are innovative and open to change, and who are able to express the nuances and abstract truths of our faith in an accessible, popular way. It seems to me that the Province is very much the kind of community that is ready for the kind of encounter that Pope Benedict had in mind. Not only do we have in our bones the old scholastic maxim, *quidquid recipitur ad modum recipientis recipitur*, so that we preach the Gospel in a way that it may be heard by those who listen to us. We are also the heirs of an intellectual formation and a tradition of study that is rooted in the kind of dialogue that happens in the Courtyard of the Gentiles.

We see this in the brothers who have gone before us and who questioned, probed, and looked for the truth wherever they might find it. I believe that it is in one of the windows of the old priory chapel at Fenwick High School where we see a triumphant St. Thomas, with the books of Averroes and Avicenna scattered at his feet. Probably, however, Athanasius Weisheipl or Jean-Pierre Torrell give us a more accurate depiction of St. Thomas at study, pointing out that the Angelic Doctor always kept the works of Averroes and Avicenna very near, in fact close by him on top of his desk. No trampling here. We know from Marie-Dominique Chenu how St. Thomas pondered the *auctoritates* that had had come down to him, the books of the Bible, the works of the Fathers, and of course the texts of the scientists and philosophers of his time. He could see that these *auctoritates* did not always agree with one another, and he learned how to reconcile the key statements of the faith through the new science of dialectic. Through the tension of the dialectic, through the alignment of the key texts from the tradition in a dynamic conversation with one another, he was able to create a philosophical and theological synthesis that offered a more complete vision of reality than the fragmented view of any one of the individual *auctoritates* by themselves.

What Aquinas did at Paris, Naples, and Rome, our brother Francisco de Vitoria did three centuries later at Salamanca. The experience of brothers like Pedro de Cordoba, Antonio de Monstesinos and Bartolomé de las Casas, held in tension with the theological training that had been his own, gave rise to a new and profoundly richer understanding of the human person, human society, and human rights. Again and again in our intellectual tradition, whether it is with a Catherine of Siena, a Meister Eckhart, a Marie-Joseph LaGrange, an Yves Congar, or our own St. Albert the Great, we see this same quest for truth through the long and sometimes painful process of being intellectual vulnerable to the new idea, to the new concept, to the new reality that we have encountered.

So it must be for us when we enter the Courtyard of the Gentiles. There we will find committed Christians who think differently than we do. We may see quite liberal or progressive Catholics, whatever we choose to call them, as well as Catholics whom we may regard as traditionalist, conservative, even reactionary. We will meet Orthodox Christians, Protestants, Jews, and a growing number of Muslims, Buddhists, and Hindus. In the Courtyard we will also encounter agnostics and practical atheists, men and women who are searching for meaning in their lives, who are looking for something to which they can cling, something that will provide their lives with purpose and a sense of worth. For some it is their spouses and their children, for others it is their careers and professions, the size of their stock portfolio or their pursuit of pleasure. There are those who turn to their commitments, to their service to humanity, to scientific research and technology, to the various arts, or to the academy. Still others jump from one thing to another, always looking, never finding. For many of them God is simply an after-thought if he is thought about at all. Our first impulse may be to say something, to correct errors, to provide answers, and to present the truth. Yet this desire to speak can be a temptation and even a mistake. We come to the Courtyard first in order to listen.

Although we are in the Courtyard to learn, to listen, and to sit with the other, we cannot forget that we also have something to share from our study. Dominican study can never be understood merely as an academic exercise, nor as an activity that takes place in a vacuum. As Dominicans, we study not for our own professional development, nor even for our own personal enrichment. Always we study in pursuit of *Veritas* so that we may bring what we have learned to the mission, for the sake of preaching and for the salvation of souls. Moreover, we have this confidence that we can attain Truth because we regard the world as infinitely intelligible, infinitely knowable, and infinitely accessible since we have the capacity to know and to understand. St. Augustine says in his *De Trinitate* that we are *capax Dei*. I would suggest that we are *capax Dei* because we are first *capax Veritatis*. Because we are capable of knowing the Truth, we are capable of the One who is Truth himself. Of course, in our Christian understanding, what is especially privileged as revelatory of truth is the Word of God. In our study of this Word, we come to know, we come to love, and we come to be united to the One who is Truth Himself. We study then for the same reasons that we pray, so that we might become friends of God and enter into the divine life of the Trinity.

This friendship with God, which we acquire through the study of his Word, we cannot help but share with others. So we come to the Courtyard of the Gentiles with something to bring, not only something to learn from our Dominican tradition of study. Ours is a vision that recognizes the dignity and goodness of every individual thing that exists, because each creature finds its source in God and its fulfillment in God. As Dominicans we recognize that we live in a graced world, suffering from the effects of sin certainly, but sustained and directed by a provident God, who is infinitely knowable and infinitely loveable. We are convinced that every human person has inestimable value because each of us has been made in God's image and likeness. We know that ours is a bodily nature, and we give more than grudging respect to the physical, emotional, and social needs that are so much a part of our physicality. We embrace fully our corporeality. Yet we also understand that we are more than our bodies. Our natures are also spiritual. As made in God's image, we have an intellect that is ordered to know him, the One who is Truth himself, and a will to love him, the One who is Goodness himself. We believe that we have the capacity to know this Truth and to love this Good by choosing freely with the assistance of grace and with the help of the virtues, especially the gifts of faith, hope, and love. What was damaged by sin has not only been restored but has been made even more beautiful by the life, death, and resurrection of Jesus Our Lord who has perfected the image of God in us. In the Spirit whom The Father and Son have sent, this Spirit who has united us to one another as members of Christ's body and who continues to sanctify us, we are now able to attain God, to enjoy God, and to live in the shared life of the Trinity.

Ours is an extraordinary vision of reality, one that remains essentially optimistic. We approach the world with confidence, even as we are painfully aware of its flaws and failures, because we remain convinced of its goodness. We are cognizant of our strength, despite our own sinfulness and the sinfulness that we see in others, because we are attentive to the working of grace in our midst. Despite the anxiety of the present time, always we are men who trust in the future, because we know that it is God's world and that the future belongs to the One who will be all in all. How different this vision is from that of other Christians, even from other Catholics! Too often religious culture, including Catholic culture, appears reticent about the world, suspicious of it, and defensive, finding itself embattled in what it an perceive as a life-and-death struggle with secularism, individualism, relativism, and a debased culture. This is not the Dominican way.

As Pope Francis says in his recent Apostolic Exhortation, *Evangelii Gaudium*, "Proclaiming the Gospel message to different cultures also involves proclaiming it to professional, scientific, and academic circles. This means an encounter between faith, reason, and the sciences with a view to developing new approaches and arguments on the issue of credibility and creative apologetics which would encourage greater openness to the Gospel on the part of all." (n. 132) He goes on to say, "It is not enough that evangelizers be concerned to reach each person.... A theology which is in dialogue with other sciences and human experiences is most important for our discernment on how best to bring the Gospel message to different cultural contexts and groups (n. 133). In this dialogue, Francis argues, there is a genuine need for research and scholarship, not simply in the sacred sciences but also in the secular disciplines, if we are going to understand the world in which we live and if we are going to a make a contribution to its transformation, as well as to our own.

Our Dominican understanding of study should assist us in our engagement with men and women pastorally but also with the world of science, culture, intellectual ideas, and the arts. As Dominicans our prayer and study of the Word of God offer a compelling view of the world, a profound understanding of the human person and the progress of the moral life, and an orientation toward a goal which can be attained in our knowledge and love of the One who is both Truth itself and Goodness itself. In the Courtyard of the Gentiles these perspectives will be most helpful in presenting the Good News of Jesus

Christ crucified and risen.

In order for the Province to fulfill this promise we need a vibrant Aquinas Institute of Theology committed to this vision of Dominican study. Without such a vision, we remain simply one more generic school of theology that offers the Master of Divinity with a couple of extra courses on preaching. With such a vision and with a curriculum that truly actualizes it, we prepare our students, especially our Dominican brothers, to engage in the kind of evangelization that is so necessary at the present time. Like many of you, I am aware of some of the challenges that we face with regard to our school, especially the few Dominican friars who are teaching at Aquinas. A critical mass of brothers, I believe, is necessary if we are going to be true transmitters of our Dominican intellectual tradition. It is much harder to do this when there are only a couple of us.

Moreover, it is important that our school remain intellectually rigorous. If we expect our students to possess this Dominican understanding of study and to be prepared for future doctoral studies, then they must be able to read and interpret texts and to be able to express themselves cogently. In their academic work and in their contemplative study of the Word of God, they must be enlivened and not leave Aquinas deadened and exhausted. We may be so committed to fulfilling goals and objectives and to completing a curriculum required by accrediting agencies and by the American bishops that we forget that our students have a right to be formed in the fullness of our Dominican intellectual tradition. Finally, I am also aware of the financial vulnerability of Aquinas. Here, brothers, I would say that we must try to provide as much financial support as we can. From my experience in other provinces of the Order that have their own centers of institutional formation, most contribute much more to their centers of studies than we do. To operate a center of institutional studies that will form our brothers, not first for the priesthood, but for the Order, is a major commitment that we have undertaken. Yet to my mind it is the most important commitment that we have. It calls for sacrifice on all of our parts to see that the school has the Dominican friar professors that it needs, that it possesses the financial wherewithal to fulfill its mission, and that it is able to form our brothers as men who know our intellectual tradition and who love it, so that study will be a life-long passion in their lives. This commitment I believe is essential, even if there are other good things that we may not be able to do. I am well aware that in other provinces, when their centers of studies are threatened or become vulnerable, the brothers of those provinces rally to protect their schools. With our own tradition of study in our province, I am confident that this will be our response as well. Our presence in the Courtyard of the Gentiles demands it.

I do not pretend that it is easy for any of us to venture into the Courtyard of the Gentiles. To be there requires intellectual honesty and humility. It means that we seek to constructively engage those whom we might prefer to ignore and even to demonize. It demands that we look at them in a new way, as men and women who may have something important to say to us and who can help us come to a deeper grasp of the truth. It also requires from us a genuine commitment to study, to learn about the world in which we live, and to examine critically how contemporary thought patterns, the economic system, scientific advances, the appeal of traditional Catholicism, and current forms of atheism and agnosticism influence those around us. We will have little to contribute to a discussion on ecumenism, to a panel on interreligious dialogue, or to a conversation on the economy, immigration, or atheism, if we are unaware of the key issues, the *status quaestionis*, and the continuing neuralgic points. It goes without saying that it is not sufficient for us to speak dogmatically about issues in which we have had no formal training, or where our acquaintance with a topic is limited to a column that we saw in the *New York Times* or an article that we read on Wikipedia.

Life in the Courtyard demands serious, dedicated, and sustained study. At the same time, it requires a profound understanding of our own faith, one that we continue to acquire through our reading of Scripture, the Fathers and Doctors of the Church and contemporary theologians. This will enable us to make the necessary distinctions, to appreciate the nuances, and to be able to separate what is constitutive of our faith from those things that are transitory and not essential. It means also that we remain grounded firmly in prayer and in the common life that we share. For true though it is that we come to the Courtyard in order to learn and to pursue the truth, we come also to proclaim our faith in Christ. As Pope Francis puts it, "true openness involves remaining steadfast in one's own deepest convictions, clear and joyful in one's own identity, while at the same time being "open to understanding those of the other party and knowing that dialogue can enrich each side" (n. 196). Without this clarity, without this purpose, without this *raison d'être*, we will be simply one more voice in the Courtyard.

Globalizing American Catholics [GACs]: The Continuing Relevance of the Dominican Vocation

Scott Appleby, Ph.D.

I am honored to be invited to address this anniversary assembly 75 years after the founding of the province of St. Albert the Great, 192 years after Bishop Fenwick established the first American Dominican missionary presence in Kentucky and Ohio, and 798 years after Dominic of Osma established the Order of Preachers. He did so in response not only to false preaching by heretics in southern France that was leading miserably poor people to deny the goodness of God's creation, but to ineffectual **orthodox** preaching by fellow Catholics. It would be unseemly of me to name names so let me simply read this account from *The Catholic Encyclopedia*: "The Cistercians, on account of their worldly manner of living had made little or no headway against the Albigenses. They had entered upon their work with considerable pomp, attended by a brilliant retinue, and well provided with the comforts of life."

This would not do for Dominic, who as a student had once sold his possessions, including precious scholarly manuscripts, to help feed the hungry. "Would you have me study off these dead skins," he asked his incredulous fellow students, "when men are dying of hunger?"

I open with my remarks this vignette so that we might ponder together this evening the persisting relevance of Dominic's question. *How are we* to meet the challenge of integrating study with service, preaching with practice, contemplation with action? This unlikely feat of integration has been the special charism of the Order of Preachers, from the time Dominic made history by leaving the seclusion of the rural monastery for the accessibility of the urban priory, by creating a new kind of modern apostle called the friar, and by founding a religious community that raised both the art of mystical prayer and the science of university learning to unprecedented heights.

The challenge to which the Dominicans have responded for nearly 800 years is today a challenge that must be met by religious and laity alike, by Dominicans, Franciscans, Jesuits—and, yes, those American Cistercians, the Trappists—but also and increasingly by lay communities and lay professionals "living in the city" close to those to whom they minister. Lay as well as religious must continue to be nourished by prayer, by the rosary, by what Meister Eckhart called the "God beyond God"—the One who shatters the illusions thrown up by our meager imaginations and who masters us with incomprehensible Love.

Taking up the Dominican mantle is required of all serious Christians in our day. The persistence of poverty, the scourge of genocide, the spreading globalization of the slave trade and human trafficking, the millions of people living in refugees camps at bare subsistence levels—and yet the inattention and spiritual somnolence of millions of privileged North Americans living in comfort, not least many among the younger generations. How can we study off these dead skins when men, women and children are needlessly suffering and dying in unacceptable numbers every day?

Hope arising

Just as Dominic burst upon the scene unexpectedly to capture the imagination of his contemporaries, so too has another man of compassion and mercy rekindled our spiritual lives and moral imagination. Like Dominic, Pope Francis eschews the trappings of wealth and power, speaks from a heart softened and strengthened by forgiveness, enjoins and enacts practices of mercy and compassion, speaks truth to power, and embraces the miserable while proclaiming the glory of God and the created world.

And how does this alienated, suffering, confused but still somehow hopeful church and world respond? With amazed delight! With eagerness to receive the latest from the Vatican! With pilgrimages to Rome to greet this spiritual successor of Dominic (and of Francis, and Catherine of Siena, and Bernard of Clairvaux, and Ignatius). *Can we believe this? Can we hope this spirit of renewal will prevail?*

Certainly there is a receptive audience, not least among the cohort of young Americans I know best: the students and recent graduates of the University of Notre Dame. I am also keeping track of studies by social scientists such as David Yamane and Christian Smith, who analyze the ideas and behaviors, sensibilities and aspirations of young Americans coming to personal maturity, from high school seniors in their late teens to postgraduates in their thirties.[34] Of the many characteristics defining these younger generations, I should like to focus on their keen awareness of the world—specifically, of being "connected" to one another across continents, of being "in touch" via technology and travel, and, most important, of standing "in solidarity" with people oppressed by poverty, violence and discrimination of all sorts.

Studies show that younger Americans, especially the large minority who go on from high school to community colleges or universities, are increasingly knowledgeable about and interested in "global affairs" and of the struggles of people in what were once called "far-away foreign lands"—places like Egypt, Iraq, Syria, Brazil, Japan, China and the Philippines. A subset of this subset, represented especially by students enrolled in Catholic institutions of higher education, bring to this greater global awareness a conscience and consciousness formed by engagement with Catholic social teaching.

These young seekers and do-ers—let us call them **"globalizing American Catholics"** [GACs] embody the answer to a question that has dogged Catholic preachers and professors since the waning of the initial renewal sparked by the Second Vatican Council: How might we rekindle (or kindle) the spark of fervor— intellectual, spiritual, moral and psychological—which animated previous generations of Catholic youth? For many of us who took seriously our identity as aspiring Catholic intellectuals as we earned our doctorates in the 1980s and early '90s, the irony today is that we lamented what we thought at the

---

[34]Christian Smith with Kyle Longest, Jonathan Hill and Kari Christoffersen, *Young Catholic America: Emerging Adults In, Out of, and Gone From the Church*(Oxford University Press, 2014); Christian Smith, *Lost in Transition: The Dark Side of Emerging Adulthood* (Oxford University Press, 2011); David Yamane, *Becoming Catholic: Finding Rome in the American Landscape* (Oxford University Press, 2014).

time was the scarcity of Catholic intellectuals on the American scene. We did not know how good we had it! Our question now is not "Where are today's Catholic Salks, Einsteins and Oppenheimers," but where are today's Thomas Mertons, Walker Percys, David Tracys, Andrew Greeleys?

Besetting social sins threaten to dampen the enthusiasms of the young. The twin crises of 9/11 and the sexual abuse scandal deflated the Catholic imagination of the generation now in their late 20s and early 30s; fewer of them are eager to apply their Catholic university educations to Catholic matters.

There is a silver lining, however. From my perch as a Catholic educator and director of a peace studies institute with affiliations to numerous such institutes, centers and networks around the world, I see evidence that a convergence of social trends and new intellectual resources has created a platform for the reinvigoration of the Catholic apostolate to the young, through the cultivation of GACs. These socially concerned, globally aware youth wish to **study and celebrate and heal** "the world"—a world wracked by sin, violence and death, and yet suffused by grace, and sustained by hope in the redemptive presence of the Holy Spirit.

The World of the GACs

A practical, pragmatic generation, GACs are intrigued by concepts and theories only as they are embedded in concrete social settings and grounded in social practices. These practices constitute a **discourse of global justice**. Generation Google, as the larger cohort is sometimes called, takes for granted a condition of interdependency, in which the fate of peoples scattered across vast expanses of space are intertwined as never before, in which the challenges humankind faces are entangled, mutually constituted and conditioned. It is a world where initiatives toward economic development and the provision of basic health care must unfold amidst climate change and resource wars, in which solutions must be elicited from local cultures as well as from transnational organizations, in which syncretism and pluralism has become the default mode of social interaction.

Such a world is always in danger of fragmenting, of descending into the anarchy of multiple solipsisms. Generation Google's wariness of isolation and disconnectedness explains why its emerging leaders are ever busy building platforms for collaboration. (Bill Gates is one of the revered elders of this generation.) The GACs, like their generational peers, linger less on discerning philosophical, epistemological or theological foundations for unity. But they share with their Catholic parents and grandparents an abiding dedication to pursuing the question of meaning.

What is new in this world? Certainly the mixing, matching and blending of religious and secular and ethnic and cultural practices and discourses has always been a byproduct and feature of human interaction, as has the condition of plurality. Yet for today's GACs it is precisely "the awareness that we are all in one single, global humanity living in the same time and space" which is radically new. The eminent Catholic sociologist of religion, Jose Casanova, argues that despite previous eras of transnational mobility and encounter, only ours can rightly be called the "age of globalization," for "it is an age in which we all, whether we want to or not, become consciously aware of globalization, both in terms of global connectivity—everything that happens affects everybody else in the globe—and global consciousness. This combination of connectivity and consciousness is indeed a new condition which we all must take into account."

The combination of consciousness and connectivity has created new and bracing "plausibility structures" for younger generations—material, institutional and psychological conditions within which it is possible to imagine and enact not merely truly global commerce and intellectual exchange but also person-to-person, group-to-group interaction and collaboration for the common good. Transformational professional partnerships on a global level are increasingly viable not merely for major multinationals and governments but for a cohort of young peace, justice and development activists—including Catholics who embrace the notion and goals on integral human development.

Boston College theologian and ethicist Lisa Sowle Cahill has recently explored this convergence of social trends and intellectual resources. She proposes a development of Christian ethics inspired by the inculturation of the gospel around the world, a process that is driven by actual on-the-ground contact and collaboration with a range of religious and secular actors in Africa, Asia and Latin America. (Our GACs will seek to engage with and even join this company of actors.) Cahill calls upon American Catholic leaders to stimulate what she calls "a twenty-first-century Christian response to the Global realities of human inequality, poverty, violence, and ecological destruction—a response that can link the power of the gospel to cross-cultural, cross-generational and interreligious cooperation for change."[35]

At the center of Cahill's vision is the claim that "the sociopolitical dimension of salvation has consequences for the purposes and criteria of theology." Thus she examines how the symbols of God, nature, creation and atonement function in concrete global settings of poverty and violence; and she feeds theory by constant references to peace-building and justice practices, in an effort to make "a neo-pragmatist case for the practical character of truth claims." Hers is an engaged theology, an ethics for a globalizing world caught in spirals of economic underdevelopment, deadly conflict and not least the daily and horrific violation of the bodies of both women and men.[36]

Cahill's project stands in historical continuity with American Catholic traditions of global engagement and practical theology dating back at least to the formation of Maryknoll at the turn of the twentieth century. By relocating these traditions within a global, gendered, multireligious setting, however, she points to the possibilities of transformation of traditions fostered under the influence of a set of cultural and political assumptions accompanying postwar American triumphalism with its attendant nationalist and neo-colonialist over-tones.

---

[35] Lisa Sowle Cahill, *Global Justice, Christology and Christian Ethics*. (New Studies in Christian Ethics. Cambridge: Cambridge University Press, 2013). In developing this proposal, she retrieves core insights from the Catholic intellectuals of our formative golden years—Gustavo Gutierrez and Jurgen Moltmann, David Tracy and Beth Johnson; but she also draws on a contemporary array of developing world theologians and peace and justice practitioners in several countries across the globe, such as Wonhee Ann Joh, Marilyn McCord Adams, and Takatso Alfred Mofokeng.
[36] This discussion of Cahill's work is excerpted from my essay in a forthcoming volume edited by James Heft and Una Cadegan..

Cahill's final chapter reflects systematically on her engagement with Catholic peacebuilders from Mindanao, Colombia and Great Lakes Africa. Composed in the form of an invitation to aspiring Catholic activists to match their zeal for real-world engagement with intellectual inquiry, the final sentences set forth the outlines of a new agenda for Catholic engagement: "Peacebuilders are respectful of distinctive identities that lead to different worldviews, practices, and priorities. Yet they are also convinced that people everywhere value basic respect, access to the essential conditions of a dignified life, political participation, and social organization that facilitates peaceful coexistence. For peacebuilders, the politics of salvation moves from local communities of faith to regional and global societies, joining Christian faith with experience of God in other religious traditions."

Can the Dominicans Meet Their Part of the Challenge?

What has this expansive vision to do with the next phase of Dominican witness and ministry in North America? That, in part, could become a topic for your reflection and discussion. But let me close by gesturing toward some of the possibilities.

From the population of Catholic as well as non-Catholic teens and young adults living in the province—including, of course, the many thousands of students enrolled in St. Louis high schools and colleges—you might aspire to cultivate a subset which could eventually comprise a cohort of lay Catholic "ministers" and "apostles."

In this context "ministry" and "apostolate" are to be understood as refashioned around a global imaginary. Dominicans must draw unto themselves young adults who can be formed and then "dispatched bearing the good news" to their professional peers with expertise in health care, conflict mediation, human rights, economic development, grassroots political activism, educational reform and the like. Whatever the career trajectories of these potential lay ministers and apostles and their peer audiences, they will likely emerge within both national and international frames of reference. So, too, must the proclamation of the gospel by Dominicans and your lay brothers and sisters. The kerygma must be fashioned in such as way as to engage this new global imagination. Domestic crises in our own cities are now conceptualized and will be solved within a global horizon; so, too, must the Christian message of love and compassion be cast within the horizons of potentially engaged Christian youth who, in their professional lives, are struggling to foster unity within diversity, to craft programs for those left behind in the global economy, and for victims of urban, gang and political violence.

Imagine a cohort of Dominican-influenced young men and women who will serve in government, in nongovernmental organizations and in the private sector, crafting alternatives to environmental degradation, militarism, exploitation of the labor force, government inefficiency and corruption, and other pressing, globalized social, economic and political challenges. Ensuring the "Dominican influence" is a formidable task, I realize, but it is one commensurate with your history, mission and charism. It will take strategic planning and indefatigable leadership to leverage your current strengths and gifts, to build a legacy for a lay-led future.

There is no doubting the need for "proclamation" emerging from faith, grounded in learning and articulated in the popular idiom. As in the past, the Dominican vocation to "sacred study and preaching" remains relevant—especially if it is re-imagined along the lines I have suggested. We Catholic professors know firsthand that a vital, moral, imaginative and relentless generation of young Americans is being unleashed upon unsuspecting colleagues and superiors. This is seen, among other places, in the proliferation of human rights organizations, relief and development agencies, and peacebuilding NGOs. Role models abound, from Pope Francis to the Dalai Lama, to Bill Gates. A new generation offers genuine promise for rekindling the national and global moral imagination—and for renewing the church.

It is appropriate, perhaps, that I end this exhortation about meeting the demands of a digitally connected age by quoting from your website! So listen to what *you* say about the continued relevance of your "preaching":

> *Our common life, our study and our prayer are all geared to support the vocation of a preacher. For us*

preaching takes many forms. We preach from the pulpit during liturgy and at retreats, but we also consider our teaching and various kinds of pastoral care to be ways in which we bring the healing Word of God to bear on the lives of those we serve. Our preaching ministry takes us to parishes, university campuses, retreat centers and sometimes even to food pantries, shelters for the homeless and other places where people are impoverished literally as well as spiritually.

Need I say it? That is where the GACs are waiting for you.

www.ingramcontent.com/pod-product-compliance
Lightning Source LLC
Chambersburg PA
CBHW061302040426
42444CB00010B/2477